Champions

By Sally Cowan

Have you ever entered a contest?
Did you win a prize?

You can do all kinds of amazing things to win prizes and be a champion.

You could run the fastest or be the smartest.
You could even tell the funniest joke or do the trickiest magic trick!

Fest

These kids are good at solving this mini cube game. They are being timed!

They need to match up all the colours on the mini cube, and they must be the quickest.

The quickest kid to finish is the champion.

SPEED
STACKS

SPEED

Some kids tell the funniest jokes at Joke Fest.

The other kids vote for the best joke.

Lin told a funny joke about a mosquito inside a piano.
She was the champion of Joke Fest!

Some kids enter speech contests.

Lisa gave a speech about people who go deep into the sea in submarines to study marine life. It's like an underwater safari!

She spoke very well, and she won a prize!

Dion and his band are in a music contest.
His band hopes to be the champions and win first prize.

Dion had to catch a taxi in his band uniform!

Luke learned about a kids' baking contest on the radio.

He spent the day baking treats with a bit of chilli in them.

He hopes to win the top prize.

Mia loves to garden, so she entered the flower contest at the town fiesta.

She would love to win the prize for the best flowers.

Mia will need to look after her flowers very well until the day of the contest.

My mum was a champion skier. She won lots of medals in ski contests.

She teaches me how to ski now.

Maybe one day I will win a prize, too!

Pets can also win prizes.

My pet corgi wins the race!
He is the champion!

CHECKING FOR MEANING

1. Who was the champion of Joke Fest? *(Literal)*
2. What did Luke hope to win a prize for? *(Literal)*
3. Is the mum on page 12 still a champion skier? How do you know? *(Inferential)*
4. Which contest from the text would you most like to win? Why? *(Evaluative)*

EXTENDING VOCABULARY

champion	What does it mean if you are the champion of something?
marine	What does the word *marine* refer to? What is another way the author could have described the topic of Lisa's speech?
spoke	What tense is the word *spoke*? How would you say this in the present tense? What other words have a similar meaning to *spoke*?

MOVING BEYOND THE TEXT

1. Which of the activities mentioned in the text are you good at? Are you good at any other activities? Tell me about them.
2. How can you prepare for a competition?
3. Why is it important to practise when you are part of a team, like Dion in his band?
4. Would you like to be the judge (or referee or umpire) for a competition, game or activity? Why?

TIME TO WRITE

Imagine you are preparing for a contest. What contest would you enter? What do you do to get ready? How do you feel on the contest day?